I, IN THE
MEMBERSHIP
OF MY DAYS

I, IN THE
MEMBERSHIP
OF MY DAYS

poems by

RICHARD
HARRIS

London
Michael Joseph

First published in Great Britain by Michael Joseph Ltd
52 Bedford Square, London WCI
1975

ISBN 0 7181 1371 3

Printed in Great Britain by
Hollen Street Press Ltd at Slough, Berkshire
and bound by James Burn at Esher, Surrey

Dedicated to

Harriet-Mary
who
is still in my
heart

and

Flanny
who
is still in my
head

*Requiem Aeternam dona eis, Domine,
Et Lux perpetua Luceat eis.*

CONTENTS

PROLOGUE

I, IN THE MEMBERSHIP OF MY DAYS

July 1970

I
in the membership of my days
stand
outside the farthest heartbeat
of my nearest member
cracking in love
breaking beyond my point
seeing the stones
in my heart
part
my waters without end
shading shadows on my dearest tomb
too early in my fall

I
who broke my own
lie
broken in the laughter of my game
lives sideways
Inside out and outside in
upside down
in the empty town
of my own making
call out clear
in the lighthouse harbour
sail in deafness
afraid an answering call
too proud in shipwrecked fields
to grasp the saving line

I
born from a cubic womb
hammered
my shape to ring circles
around the moon of my genesis
blazing unending fight
across the jaded cobwebbed
living rooms
stirring lives to light
grassing endlessly
in flashbulbed streams of honour
ceased to flow as nature drew
wrapped on pulp and tissue
as useless as it was helpless

I
who lay inside me
sleeping
daylong hungry hours
suspecting the tired impulses of my feelings
sought all things uneasy
in the easy streets of recompense
reconciled with myself
turning my cheek
in a narcissistic blow
falling headlong into my own charity

I
who was sin
began
committing myself
When bread was first broken
on the pubic altar of my greed
waited for love too long
too late in the forty years of my sun
to run again in fancy speed
to seek a hideout for my seed
Unlike others
bought the book
made the rules
committing offenses
in the board room of my desire

I
who was stone
carved
my grief in granite
heaving the rock to shoulder
bolder than my step
strode in march and willow bank
sank to the height of my weight
too smart to see
the stupid on my back
flung out days in waste
stripping the calendar of my years

I
who was father and son
children
to my theme
retarded the spirit in my flock
staged in the theatre of my orphanage
blank in the make-up mirror
doctored the lines across the stained glass
painting suggestions
on images without reflections
trying to make visible
lines that were invisible
and never really there

I
who was earth
fathered
my own bone
running from the sound and fragrance
of touch and taste
failed to sight
the apocalypse in my marrow
having no beginning
saw no end
failed to comprehend
the shapeless space
running through the gaps in my mould

I
who was Lazarus
beggar
in my rich
waited in my tomb
fighting shafts of restoring light
lying in needless numb
locked out the air
weaved in death a canopy
sheltering my rest from miracles
sang requiems to my skeleton
black as the mass I served in my offer

I
who was
I
without
me
cannot recall living
was from the beginning
born
dead

YESTERDAY

long
long
ago

POEMS 1939-1946

B

I CRIED ALL NIGHT

1939

I cried all night
last Tuesday
and can't remember why
but I do remember why
I was smiling on Wednesday morning
the things you remember are the best

MY SISTER HAD A DOG

1939

My sister had a dog
named Reggie
she loved Reggie
she said she loved me too
she kissed and patted Reggie
she never kissed and patted me
yesterday night I ran
around the house barking
and my father hit me

MY YOUNG BROTHER

1939

My young brother
was in his pram
I walked along beside him
he looked so white and peaceful
he also looked so warm
I wonder if I'll ever
be that small again

HE SAT ALONE

1940

He sat alone and ate
he walked alone and thought
he heard of beauty lone he sought
he found happiness alone and smiled
he dreamt alone and toiled
he felt sadness alone and cried
he loved alone and died

I WROTE AS TOLD

1942

I wrote as told
to Santa Claus
because I wanted many many
things for Christmas

Dear Santa Claus
I want many many things for Christmas
a real flying aeroplane
a real horse like Trigger
that comes when whistled at
real guns that kill
a real car
not too big
that won't hit the lane gate
if I drive home drunk
like Daddy
well
that is all unless you can think of anything I need
God bless you
Dickie

I got my plane
I got my horse
I got my gun
I got my car

But maybe next they'll be real
like I wrote and asked for
but it doesn't matter
Daddy said
"if they're wrapped in love
then they are really real"

But the important thing is
I flew my plane to Egypt
rode my horse against indians
shot all the bad men
drove my father home every night
without hitting the lane gate once
and although you never thought
of anything else I might need
it doesn't matter
because Daddy was right
my presents were wrapped with love

OUR GREEN HOUSE

1942

Our green house
was where Beau Geste
ran to
deep in the desert

Our gooseberry bushes
was where
I ambushed all the Wells Fargo's

Our apple trees
was where
I played Tarzan
with my neighbour (Sally)
(She wasn't as pretty as a Maureen O'Sullivan
but I forgave her when she rescued
me from the hungry crocodiles)

The plum tree
was where
(it wasn't our plum tree but the branches
hung over the wall into our garden)
I boarded the Spanish ship
and saved the British Empire

Our pear tree
was where
I saved Sally from the giant

The pole
that kept the Monday washing up
was my
brother's own surrender flagpole
(Mum was angry when
he used my sister's knickers as a white flag)

The garage
without the car
was where
I judged the bad
and was judged when bad

The garage
with the car
was the plane
I bombed the Germans from
the ship I captained
the tanks I drove
the stagecoach I killed
Geronimo from
he died five times
(My brother said I was a lousy shot
the truth was that he was a bad loser)

The outside toilet
was the electric chair
(I didn't like that game
although I got to play James Cagney)

Our lane
was where I captained Ireland
against England at Rugby
kicked endless goals
was carried off the field
shoulder high
by my thousands of fans
and called the greatest ever
I
won everything my heroes won
in our lane
I was the greatest ever
until I took a bath
then I was me again
the middle son in a family of eight
wearing my elder brothers'
hand-me-downs

Our house
was where
my mum and dad lived
and at night
it was the happiest place
I'd travelled all day

I RAN AWAY

1943

I ran away
I ran far away
from home again
the nights were empty
so was my tummy
I came home
I came home
from far away again

I sneaked up the lane
climbed the wall
and saw my father
still practicing golf
and saw my mother
still knitting away
and saw my brothers
still going on dates
and saw my sister
still kissing Reggie (her dog)

I ran away for nothing
I'll try again tomorrow

1945

Mum was crying on the phone
her green eyes
pouring
out some sorrow

I wanted to touch her
and
shield her eyes
from the things her ears were hearing

But I didn't
somehow
I understood
that her sorrow was private
and sharing it
would only make it doubly worse

LIMERICK 245
(Reverse Charge)
1945

Dad was crying on the phone
his blue eyes
pouring
out some sorrow

I wanted to touch him
and
close his mouth
from the things that he was saying

I tried
somehow I understood
when he waved me away
I suppose he was right
I was really far too young
to be of any help

THOUGH I KILLED THE BIRD

1946

Though
I killed the bird
I hadn't heard
its cry of peace in the scarlet score
of my own game

Perched unaware
on the branch of its own maim
in a negative day
caught
in the officious way
of my worm and trap
I cast
my hammer into his winter song
and saw it stammer and stall
and fall on the retail of the earth's lap

Robin red and tender breast
burst in my time
on the prime of the white-faced snow
below
the aim and lame of my youth
armed
in the truth I now behold
I scold
myself

———

YESTERDAY

not so
long
ago

POEMS 1947-1957

MY BLOOD REFLECTS NOTHING OF ME

1952

My blood
reflects nothing of me

It reflects
beer
whiskey
guinness
lack of passion
or
passion held by catholic beads

It moves in circles
through my tree
unrooted to my earth
each drop in siege
and careless in having
no relationship to my body

But when I bleed
it belongs to her
only then
it is a part of me

HONEYMOON ON SIXPENCE

January 1957

Honeymoon
on sixpence

Food unfed
before
the virgin bed
we already lay open on

Time
would turn back the sheets
on the phallic
stage of communion
but
not before we touched
the numbered beauty
in our hidden cell

The bread and wine
would
turn sour and stale
before
our risen godbody turns into clay

Holy
on our break fast night
my virgin
waiting to be ripped
in the thunder of unity
bleeds
in the chastity of our soul
chained togetherness

Before
the feast
before my dishevelled pagan
touched the mother of your church
before
my uncommon
became common in flight
before
the walk across the january park
before
the birds sang in nightingales square
before
the black world ran mad
horses over our desire
and
let loose our
reins in full

Before
the
before
before I said
I
loved in knowing you

You were gone

Loose
on a shilling spree
where
my sixpence
died
unspent

YESTERDAY

ever
present

POEMS 1958-1972

THE BLIND CHILD

May 1960

Path hidden
world ridden
wise
the child walked
in the silence of her looking-glass eyes
broken before birth

Blinded beyond grief
her world-weary stare
stored no thief
no
sawdust gift
plucked from the christmas wand
of her yearly tree

Back in her blackout days
without rainbow hail
or snowdrift sun
she inhaled dried air
grew nurseries of shapes
shaped them
into boxes
of paint
as faint
as visible

Mounting the safari
in her mind
she drew visions to her need
feeding
the blank spots
with lines
as delicate as grace
and placed
them on the mantled peace
of her burning night light

Her lines
grew alive
lived
in her knighthood
lighting the dark lanes
with
traced faces of her own

No pallid faces
stitched in aged lines
no frowns crossing
the smooth of an angel-made surface

Flowers steamed
in celestial spheres
their
arms
wrung upwards
to the root
deep in her joy
drooping
petals
to the carpet
beneath her feet

Black into white
wouldn't go
was the topic
in the arithmetic
of our world

but

black into white
was midnight into noon
with fountains of room
in the geography
of her world

Green was red
red was white

White was black
black was white

White was blue
blue was black

Black was gray
gray was nothing

Nothing was something
she never heard of

Sounds as sharp as bare
stare
at her stings
wings
into her silent crypt
devotions
peeling in templed seas
golden in mountain streams
moulded in her art
music in her want
across the virgin screens in her ears

Traffic in symphonies
cords of spring
rushing
past dead sockets
to the retainer pocket
in her head
snowflakes in wisps
whirled in essence
and
God
grew on the beaks of birds
singing
the kiss of peace
on the lips in her heart

Death
and dying
was a place
an out-of-focus face
borrowing no sorrow

Empty spaces in her hand
words
without lying eyes
departure without goodbyes
speeches from houses
white as mocking
rocking
horse of peace
in a world
she grew without

Life was a word
heard
lived in Braille

Tinker Bell and Winnie
books without jungles
Sinbad and his sailor
Gulliver
on his travels
in plastic dots
raised
to the eyeballs in her finger tips
grasping
grass and hoppers
dandelions on daisy chains
cups of buttered posies
full
of whit-chat tales
like snails
she draws
draws them into her darkened shell
and
weaves her sun

And

The blemished fossils in her earth
grew
rainbows from the crock of her gold

In her old
undeceived by concealment
still half-born
with stick and dog
barefoot
on the heated sands of her desert
her phoenix rose
lived another blood beat
in the hearts that read her testament

If we
in our cries
offered her our eyes
would she have had more vision?

THE BRAY OF MY ANIMAL

April 1966

The bray of my animal
cries out and about
dying
in the lilac haze and blue hollow on the earth's bowels
cracks the smile of the summer crust
split in the join the ceiling of my joy
blew my heaven from its holy well
to the parched desert of a loveless limbo
downed the thorned head of my pride

Dead all love and innocence
and parted the union of tomorrow and today
and too late in the lost sun
I crawl around the dead harvest of my desire
await the sledge and final blow upon my seed
what was wrong to shake my calm beyond control?
the fingers of my bent and brain box
can no longer grasp the meaning of this bleed

Here from my hunch
and middle of my howl and cripple
I cannot find the mend or see the truth of this fall
in the hush and cuddle of the madness
was the love like air and not deep rooted in the earth's grasp?
were those blessed and blistered may lips
intent to give or only to receive?
how did we cut our angel wings in the clear of its flight

Could it be
oh
could it
that in the dark and desperate of our want
we were like blindfold innocence
struck by a close thief
who with a forked and honeyed tongue
burst our bag of tears
and drowned us both in the sea of our own salt?

THIS SEPTEMBER

1967

This September
I remember

seeing my virgin love swinging
on the weeping hammock
of a borrowed willow tree
caught her infidelity shining
between the wilting whining
limbs and revealing branches
saw her swinging
heard her sinning

Clasped in a stranger's gaze
handcuffed to his mind
behind her blush
the wide flame and nostrils of his fingers
melted the sealing wax of her virginity
spinning her global orbit into dizzy
battlements of untutored joy
too long in her growth
eager to explore the passing of flesh
she glided her ribboned kite
above the watching martyr in my head
to the slave and might
of this outsider's mounting pilgrimage

Too long and too high
on my pedestal to knock
in early growing years
too pure to mix the purity
in her blood with common adam groups
too long a tenant in my shrine
too much involved with me
too little understand her
misread the head and hunger in her touch

Too late now
like rain
she came
bursting like evening silk in milk
across her arched queen
calling his name to tame
and anchor her tide
to the thrashing throne of his region

Transfixed in the gutter of my watch
the gulls in my clock
flew my ticking skull
through
bond and hollow
joy and sorrow
back
to my lost and last remember
when she could have been my september

Next september
will I remember
her first surrender?

ON THE ONE-DAY-DEAD FACE
OF MY FATHER
May 1968

Can you touch me
now
With your marble lips
and increase your love?

Can you now touch me
with your dead hand
and direct me in my path?

Now can you see me
in your dead
and say "What is right"
Though you know the answer now
Now in your stillness
Pave the way of my doing

Cold thoughts in your give
creep away
and stay
in your marble walk
and cold tombstone of your stare

Rise
now
above your mound and wound
and see your son in your eye
Touch again
the fond fountain of his
flow;
Grow
in the dead and deadly of your going

Can the paint and corrupt of your image
colour the size of my want?
Can your star in its mighty walk
balk
my evolution in its stride?

Guide me
now
in your silence
Cough up one silent prayer and stare
at me again
and see the woven fabric
of your doing
bend his knee
and plea in the tired optic of your stare
a prayer
of acceptance

Father in your mound
and farther away
I stay
at marble length and cry
Hoping that by and by in your height
I might grow
in your marble sight

SHOULD I LET HER REST

June 1968

Should I
let
her rest
on her bedrock of sperm
sliding on dried fluid
to pieces
though not in peace
trafficking the lecherous waves
washing her male stud breasts
cueing the homing pigeons home
to rest in her
splintered sighing thighs
filling nests
with eggs
from strangers' yolks
smashing shells
aborting in speed
spinning on gladiators' thumbs
dizzy as her dark mount rises
plucking fairy roses
root and stalk
from her innocent gardens

Should I
let
her rise
again naked in her cloth
habit in excess
stripped of pride
bare in loneliness
rare in beauty
wriggling on bait
hooked to promises
grinding out on stones
the hollow in her heart
selling out in heaves to thieves
her virgin album days
now
bedridden
and exposed
once sacred on shelves
outside age
growing green in preserve
recording virginity
in our asphalt growing
century's jungle

Should I
not
be kind
rewind her style
love banks full in credit
rings wisdom bells
echoing in honoured sheets
days of her nightly queen
along the cupid waters of her ethic
touching hearts in toasts
raising towers
from the arks of faith
white as clean
gentle as moonglow

Lady on your lily lilac boy
magic sail without season
sailing under golden helms
sail back
to waters in your child
you're not too soiled
to sail again

TODAY I SAW

August 1969

Today I saw
myself reflected in a millstream

Dead trees stood on dejected leaves
dead leaves kissing rooted feet
dead feet held a stranded heart
dead heart without coffins
dead coffins dying in song
dead song from marble lips
dead lips repelling kisses
dead kisses without colour
dead colour in a moving rose
dead rose on a tiny thorn
dead thorn from a loving year
dead year after you
dead you and a dying me

Today I saw
a millstream reflecting a dead face

WHAT NOW? WHAT

November 1969

What now ?
what

To unclean waters
shapeless
without means of end
to evenings spent entangled amongst the roots
of out-of-season blooms
to crushed
creased sheets
beds
where our heads
fell in whispers
behind the dawn and restless whimpers
to barren antics
where our nights spread
shed relics of our saint
in the manhood of our kind
to the centuries in our need
dead
behind the smiles and blind
of history throwing stones
to the grand
sons
daughters of our rays
burnt out
before our first draft
and tale was sold
to the broken limbs
cripple in the words
that stuttered and blasphemed
the heart's confessional

What now?
when

The eyes
of this experience will open
in a dead bare stare
thrust me back
to haunt and graze
the roundabout days
in this happening

What now?
when

Alone
alone in my groan
the deadly peace of having sketched
scratched
your depth
clings
brings forth the mirrored face
of a fast
futile life
when ghosts
pulse of evening dreams
screams
unveils the angel in your bells and singing

bringing
you back to life
leaving me
to roar
roar
at the closed door of your going

What!

Shall this jumble
muted half-baked heart
rest
on the shelves of his rival's bed
'tis best
he unwinds the grief
to the open seas
streetcar of his days
with skeleton hands and
bury his parched pain
'tis easy
to shuffle on
blind-eyed
dumb
on the run from an ever-present past
stumbling
on a grey
growing beard
feared
a dead memory will stir the dust
from the cracked
dry dock of your settle

What then?
when

The darkness
opens blackout curtains of its pores
pours
glimpses of healing light
upon the cold
long bored bones
of your living dead

Then
let my burnt-out meteor
soar across
my loss
and livelong time of thirst
burst into burnt-out fragments
all living traces
faces
finger telling touching tips
trips
to midnight cradle
tits
that once was life

And then
again

To stare
the pregnant air
shed
dead and dying thieves
upon the bare grass
gross
of my tumble-down days
ways
clutching
fistfuls of time
stretch the ages of my living

What now?
then
let

Your break
broken game
remain
like insane
children erected in the moment long
mountain tower
as thanksgiving

TIME FLIES

July 1970

Time flies
it flies timelessly
into a page of nothingness

Strangers touch
with touching hands
touchingly
a deep meeting
fleeting time
disentangles
gentleness
pushing fingers into memory
nothing will remain
only
the warm planted wild-flowers of impression
a glow in winter
a love song sung in the palm
reflections of a distant future
mirrored in today's yesterday
time
washes
nothing is removed
it only dries the fingertip tears
that smears
the ripe departure

The wild and free
running
of joy
gives birth to the girlboy
of the future
running still in timeless
days
when hands are empty
and
fingers reach out from moving doors
and pained windows
unreciprocated
where
the frost in the heart
thaws
in the old age of memory's house

WHEN I SEE IN MY FEEL

In Memory of My Sister Harriet-Mary
August 1970

When I see in my feel
the pictures of your history
fade with the sailboats of my mind

When I feel in my see
the painted foot and print of your walk
turn wild from waste

When I see
the glowing limbs of the earth
turn cripple in our ashes

When I feel
the nightmare lips of night
cannot pray for day

When I see
all blinded knees bend
make free the mercy in their hearts

When I feel
the holy waters of your font
full in the shallow of regret

When I see
the raised and promised arms of heaven
reject the holy of your visit

When I feel
two lives in one
rejecting all fathers

When I see
the sodden smoking turf
fire chimneys to the moon

When I feel
the kindergarten in your magic
rusty in your children's park

When I see
all folded shovels make crosses
on the final dead and last grave

When I see
what you have seen

When I feel
what you have felt

When I see what you have said
Then I will believe that you are dead

I AM AT SEA

August 1970

I
am the sea
singing songs from the depth
to empty vessels
floating on my head

I
am the wind
raging against the sea
singing songs
to empty vessels
floating on my head

I
am the rain
raining out the wind
raging against the sea
singing songs
to empty vessels
floating on my head

I
am the sun
burning out the rain
raining against the wind
raging against the sea
singing songs
to empty vessels
floating on my head

I
am the empty vessels
floating on my head
raged by the wind
rained by the rain
burned by the sun
sank
to the depths
to sing songs
to empty vessels
floating on my head

CHRISTY BROWN

August 1970

Christy Brown
came to town
riding on a wheelchair

Christy Brown
came to town
riding on a wheelchair

Back strapped
to wheel
and chair
free wheeling down all his days
into the
byways in our heads
visions
bursting from his pen
ink in blood
left foot in rapture
riding
through fleet street pulp
past
paper stand and paste
ploughing stairs to heaven
riding on
on
on his chariot wheels
conquering heroes in space
in the time allotted for his spin

Reared in masses
his childhood playpen on concrete slabs
turned
into flowing fountains
in his fountain pen toes
ceasing to suffer
in the kennel of his bark
spends
dark years with his ears
tied to his mother's tongue

"Where are you, Mother?"
"Here
here
I'm here, Christy
growing flowers in your yard
sending fruit to the market place
in your soul
patiently bending my breasts
to feed the hunger in your mind"

Dear Bended Lady

Drawing in midnight whispers
the elements of verse
vocalizing grammar
building his armory for battle
filling his long sleepless limping nights
with the music of her challenge
and
took a dead season from her womb
and
built a birth
as bright as christmas

In his schoolroom
slum
that buried some
crippled most
the toast from her womb
grew legs in her words
and walked
long distance to the corners of the globe
striding beyond Gethsemane
passing the avenue of sorrows
out of Golgotha
into resurrection

Christy Brown
came to town
riding on a donkey

Christy Brown
came to town
riding on a donkey

Streets in palms
carpeting
his sunday visit
rode bareback
the donkey of the apocalypse
over bridges
where crippled waters
stood still
in the lame shores of our crying
rode
heaven high
over tears and pity
through the attending city
where skeletons
hid high in the cupboards of our complacency
rode on
on
on the laughter in his sighs
everlasting in song
storming our ears in wonder
making his face
shine upon us
and
throwing from the seaweeds
of his wisdom
iodine to heal the wounds of a waiting world

BEFORE THE HIRED SPADE
In Second Memory of My Sister Harriet-Mary
September 1970

Before the hired spade
flung her final springtime
and cracked the fatal crease
in the faceless mouth of the open soil
it lingered
in telescopic silence
an octave
then shovelled into eternity
the remaining peace in our harmony

Above the hungry parlour
that housed her generations
the sackcloth back of moving
mourners moved
like a town dressed in distress
fitted out in sacramental garments
like a hive of humming bees
buzzing
in quick succession
a confession
sound of grief
their dead and deadly chords
rang out
in the empty pass of her passing
breaking the sound and barriers
of heaven
in a discordant symphony of alarm

No wish
nor brother's fame
can reclaim her now
too late in her fate
to call the wound to healing
and peeling without blood
she lies in a gesture of roses
and mocks the cushion
of her branded coffin

After the intermission of pain
I see now
though blinded in my grief
the weave in her embroidered life
stretching with every stitch
along the tresses of her design
and born in an autumn palm
widespread and giving
singing
under a slumbering serenade
along the promenade of autumn fruit
throwing out
laughter and fire
in a ferris wheel of desire
to inspire in radiance
a radius in her song

No place of grief
no thief
nor plunder
could clip assunder
her wonder in her God
though bible hand might stand
in doubt
she'd shout
out
about the mysteries that steered
the histories to compassion

Often
slipping on the frosted waters
of her reason
call the season
to bloom
in the mint and greenhouse room
watch the seed
grow
to stem
then
to flower
and shower in a magnum of vine
crying
some divine fingers dressed them
when they blessed them

Mother of two
wife to one
matriarch to an assembly
she sistered the summer flowers
in my eyes
and would disguise
them in winter
in a sense
innocence
was proud of its place
to grace the regal of her mind
and flow its rivers
along her kind
giving out tenderness

Now in this may day
forty and eight
years away
from the gate
of her birth
and first early morning
feast on earth
the light and fight in her head
fused out
to rob her of the sun
she danced her daisy chains
around in lanes
as white as sunrise

And
and
the band
of dragonflies that flew dragoons
of tales to her fancy at nursery rhyme
the pebbles peeling in her heart
the earthbound unearthly dreams
the gay smiles in blackout days
the child woman riding daft horses
wild as celtic lies
over
hinge and hinder
hoar and whore
poor and pus
over
evening lakes and morning hills
and unhealing pills
are
dead
gone
as
she
died and went
without a murmur
to outclass the class she left behind

And
in her going
the waters of my heart
burst
through the fountains of my eyes
and
day in everlasting night
my mourning kite
will fly
deep in the wilderness of my sight

BEFORE THE LIGHT
In Third Memory of My Sister Harriet-Mary
September 1970

Before the light

the candle shuffle breaks
takes the heart in concrete

Deep as death

smooth as lifeless skin
within the cage of dried bones

Hard as lily stalk

bare as the root that bore it
tore it from the womb

Bleak as blind

eyes that had no vision
decision without tongues

Nails hanging tales

curved as the cross
the loss crippled on it

Behind the priest

purple pining mothers
brothers bend in stone

Sunk in the tide

withered on the waters
daughters throw out lines

Ocean's flood in tears

evening fading light
light waits for colour

Heaven out of tune

angels singing out of range
strange when judgment calls

Husband on the verge

night calls on morning
mourning waits for silence

Breathing without life

death in the afternoon
too soon   too soon   too soon   too soon

Too soon
too soo
too so
too s
too
to
t

HARK, HAIL THE HORN BONE ON WINGS

June 1971

Wing tipped sailing soul
just
beginning to soul sail solely
connective tissue
between death and life
souring in the pouring strain of his plight
down from heaven
blazing in private passion
leaving all for granted
free
born
once
on velvet mysteries
back to the sun
ringing out joy in a hollow chest
tabernacled in faith
bare as a pauper's Christmas
everlasting in bread
hungry in his bakery
fasting in the Lent of his menagerie
crabbed in an apple cider world
bound in distilleries
adrift
between here and there
in the vast vat haunted as the orchard
seeing his knave
resting
in tinsel church towers
amongst paper-mâché men
harvesting together
and

sticking in plaster the limbs of their dreams
bowing to suffering
praising the hollow rise in a neighbor's leap
welded to consul bans
confused in the fusion
of bureaucratic crap
sighing at liberty dying
coming in wet dreams
enough to stain the mantle of the earth's potential

Malformed
in
mental
fracture
balls in rupture
apprentice to death
haggard in the braggart monster
whose mad eyes shaped lenses
in the emerald of his zoo
raped on ant hills by uncles
tossing on parents' globe
in anti-clockwise time of anti-wise
moated in trenches from advice
his base
bruised in solitude
brewed
on the unbalanced diet
over benediction fire
where his virgin lay
spliced
on the cuckold pillions of his heroes

Standing still
no more
on a putty sill of light
moulded tight
no more
on the infant train of right
rose from a bent cripple
through his stalled grill
leaving a water beetle world
skimming the surface
without submerging into depth
dug deep inside his pride
past locked-out years
deloused his head from its derelict
and
adamant as mules
reset his rock
with a government of his own
spun on a needle head
a thread of bone
weaved through his navel
a kite of ships to sail
the trumpet sounds of his own Christ

Transcended into himself

Through the chapel in his breast

Hark
hail the horn bone on wings

Gliding the rung ladder
past Eden
to the varsity of his migration
the first rudiment in a cosmic alphabet
flooded
his once
compulsory eardrums
like the magic of a day-old virgin

Hark
hail the horn bone on wings

Pounding towards the sky
easy without addresses
over
land
and
scapes
of a voodoo world
stranger to its paths
his curiosity once bound to earth
often
moored in the muddled bed of dried tradition
curls like gulls
into seasons of light
too low to hold the magic of the air

flew beyond the leafless book
of wounded teachings
to the new centuries of his heart's preserve

Hark
hail the horn bone on wings

Free
of his ordained stain
the fevered injustice
fashioned out of habit
fell
freely
from
the grace it grew in the standard
of the womb's malignancy

Hark
hail the horn bone on wings

Floating in his breast
locked in climb
above the rhyme of ferret minds
in fancy, foe and fossil
eyeing the tiny specks of human anxiety
crawling in city state
amongst concrete-mixer minds
fouling the country fowl
his shoe brain sail
trod on
over the stricken lamented earth's quake

tracking the tapestry of their travesty
sand bagged in shelter
worn as promises
loose in the storm of resurrection wine
sweat blood on the street
from bleeding feet that trapped the grape
beneath the bible heart
that throws out free anointment

Hark
hail the horn bone on wings

His harvest breast blood flows
against the spinning sail
sees the lamb grow
through his curious judgment eyes
spies
the spies in his ecclesiastic soul
ready to devour him
loose in his self-ordained hands
his trowel fingers weed out the bed head
shakes their repose
and throws
napkins to the wind
fully fused
his fire burnt dead the native warning
straight ahead his compassed passion
caught sight of the golden hair
growing
through the skull of his necessity

Hark
hail the horn bone on wings

Past
apostle James and John
through revival clouds of revelation
ploughing lonely furrows of his own text
into a light
beginning without end
growing inside
astride the tidal mind
spraying torrential questions
easing the increasing calm
burning out epitaphs of sin
casting off the grey mountain
sick rock of Peter
freeing the feet from its grim grime
inhospitable hospital below
sailing streamers around the full gloom
tourist trapping hill
swallowing his worn-out guilt
growing in the nutrition of his sin
physician and patient
confessor and confessionist
student and teacher
master and mastered

The ancient tongues that once above a time
filed an orifice through his youth
coding christian messages
as wise as penny dreadfuls
spinning toys
of cod
in an -ology of Christ
crushing credit in a free virgin membrane
grew blunt in his stride
great
as his stallion grew
shaped in size
patient to his need

Unholy he lay himself

In unholy unrest

Until his mighty formed in trust
measured in degree
to the whore he planned to play with
his standard graze
grew as cargo schooners
sailed
daily to his brain port
past scuttled years
and
tidings lettered from his God head
horizon bound in harbour wreck
the soul deep inside his eyes
sailed
inward
past
navel cord and mudflat mother virgin thighs
married himself in a honey mooned skin
watched
his foetus head grow in his sac
crying out his will
from the infant mouth of his own womb

And

Holy God
in rosary twine
held together by the three mysteries
that mastered man
in an age of numb

fell
flat
in the
free of his flying

Hark
hail the horn bone
wing tipped sailing soul
just
beginning to soul sail solely
souring in the pouring strain of his plight
down from heaven
blazing in private passion
leaving all for granted

Free
as
free
as
free
as
free
is
if
free
is
free and as free as free should be

———

AT ONE WITH ONE OCTOBER ONE

October 1971

At one
with one
october one
I
in my midnight warm
chose to be born

Feeling the art
in the artless human of my parents' hearts
grew
good in their laughter bleached beach
heard
the white in their soldier's flag
fly peace to the battle in their will
growing
comrade in the salt of their divided blood
turned
red berries into black from their green
time
wed
welded in the message of their alive

The syntax
in their undemanding flesh
needed
no form
words
it modelled itself in silence

it was
that's all
it was
and rivering through their cord
to my confinement
filled
me
with them
and
all that was theirs

Then
boarding my ship
I
decided
to sail into birth
and
grow in them and theirs
but in my grow
grew only to forget
learning to unlearn
tho'
learning too late
what I thought was mine
was only lent to give me guide

God

If only I'd stayed longer
or
hugged them more

once more
perhaps
something of their principle
might have seeded in me

Let me
then
be born
again

Them and theirs
was good

Their trumpets blew through golden candles
their single voice rang from their bosom in rejoice
their planet templed all living life
their hearts a pantheon of kneeling divinity
their spectrum clear in fullness
their simple silence quaked eternity

There was theirs
in them
from their time

Did some rub off on me?
was I too dumb to feel?
was I too numb to hear?
was I, at all anywhere?
but in myself
disregarding all that regarded my first voyage?

Shipwrecked
and
afloat
drowned in my own puberty
I
cannot visit again
the generator in their womb
or wish again
some loose sperm
rushing from their brain
might
through the dark corridors of their thighs
touch my animal

They are long dead
so is their time
so am I
and mine
and I am
as I am
now
regretting
being at one
with one
October one

FAIR EARTHQUAKE IN ONE GIVEN DAY

December 1971

Fair earthquake
in
one given day
storming my adjusted calm
re-bleeding all that lay blessed
in heaven's best
casting eyes inside
a tired worn-out scripture
republishing out-of-date volumes
of uncollected works
strident like a newborn child
years older than her years
not yet one
not yet begun
but beginning
years before my wisdom wrote a folly
she overcast my path
casting her shadow
deep inside my male

My formless map
that brought poor horizons
to the halfway house of my voyage
conjures new shapes
sees new times ticking in my compass
hears new songs singing from my wounds
sees wild unnamed orchids
growing
from the desolate of no-man's place

The unforgiving quay
that shipwrecked many dreams
glows
alight in the activity of her candle-lit waves
saves
day
from
night
like a widow out of tune in mourning

I
cannot
speed
the limit in my know
I
acknowledge all knowledge
but
I
like dumb in the manifest of your silence

Your fair earthquake
roared
in
silence
but blew great order
to the saintless border
of the heaven in my spinning
without pity
but desperate in want
I
stand

dumbfound
on the quake of my ruptured earth
calling all concealed things
to witness the testimony in my prophet

A
dislocated
heaven
touched
a
dislocated
hell
and
I
stand orphaned in limbo
Here my life-weed hands
in the masked desert
out of tune with love
stretched forth in forty christmases
yet
virgin to the feel of faithful things
sings
to
you
from the heart in the palm
and yearns to learn of gentle gospels
in the resurrection tomb of genesis

I
see no servant
in the pupil of my eye
no eclipsed moon
blowing the tides in stone
no female bait
to some biting man
bending ways to his desire

I
see a firm
of growing shapes
a wandering odyssey of colour
together growing
moulding
without question or demand
the
raped
shorelines of some infinite peace

My
scattered breathless breath of flame
claims
no plaintiff
it
stands only in the order of my second-coming
severing
the tongue

from my parched minstrel's song
that you
in your jury
might judge me
without listening to my singing
but
rather
grow
a
verdict
through the chimes in my eyes

1971

Attached
to the thatched roof
of my head
is
a splintered driftwood ghost
washed
from a storm in my past

I

in my daft
draft
the ghost
in coffin
to the tower in my dwelling

growing

in my favoured favour
it
crawls
inside my temple

tower of subsistence

between
the fixed stare of my boss-eyed sight
clawing
irregularly
at what's left of my dead patten brain
draining
my flush of life
pushing
my load of love
farther
inside my scaffold
killing
unrested corpses of rest
burning
dummy eves in beds of ice
robbing
my days of deeds
breeding
shells for devils
(the first cousins of ghosts)

The string of skin
knotting my walls of shields
protecting me
inside
from
out
rewinds
leaving my innards
sacred
from the rodent heart

The central part of my breath
craved
a hole
bigger than promises
a
slit of sixpence
high
above the thigh
beneath
the breast
between the waist
to crawl
inside
and waste my waste
forever
in a sperm flush of dust

There is no eye
in the thigh
winking me inside

now

the rocks
in the belly of my sea
grows
cousins on my head
weighing
me
for what I'm worth
until
the bone of my will
breaks
casting splinters under the feet of my sail

and

limping in terror
stare
in the recollections and reflections
of
dead-eyed Dick
casting
a
male groan as mighty as muffled mice

Headlong in reverse
speeding
backwards in neglected veins
the
ghost in my templed head
grows
towering
my half-mast life
blowing
minor keys
into daily ivory marches

and

the memory sculpture
cracks
falls
buries
its granite will
into the stained pained glass of my heart
reprinting
death
on the parapet of my soul

And

my dull eye bends in deliverance
beneath
the scythe in your brain
severing the roses in my head

and
my garden is a bleached field of crossed stone

There is nothing
more
to
do
but forge a smile in the future

I

hear the ghosts laughter

I

laugh back

uneasily

STRANDED ON ZEBRA STRANDS

1971

Stranded
on zebra strands
by traffic lights
waiting the red box
glow to green
uncalled
unknown
she came
without name
fused to my sight

One answering glance
on earth
together
the sky caught fire on our feet
the poorhouse
of our tenement
grew palaces in our blood
raining chalices on the sidewalk
all public fear
grew private
in the messenger
spinning threads
of syllables in our deaf mute sight
spiralling along
forsaken hills in rivers
dead from fasting

---

the low lone land
lying lone no longer
tossing in nakedness
calms in the eyes of love and its labors
barking in history
setting seals
the approval in our glance

Our thoughts touched
telegrams
ran through our sinewed flame
correcting faults
rewiring positives
ending blank and
cold
in corroded lines
the blessing
crossed our paths
uncovering the shelter in our ban
unafraid
friendless
potent in the indifferent street
the green waters
bathed in copulation
flushed golden
the random harvest in our fields

Outside
the world died dead
in concrete masses
office and bank
sank
knee-deep in meaningless
flowers in legions
flew from flowing streets
trees grew high from funerals
fish fed free on pavement air
mothers without wombs
grew babies in their eyes
money burnt bonfires of peace
wild girls
boys
naked outside shame
danced in rosary beaded rings
sang the blessed in their eucharist
christ without cross
hung suspended in the air

Moments on moments
days into weeks
into months into years
into centuries of love
stood still on time in trust
burst
on the winking of an eyelid

Ah
time
angry in neglect
though in good use
flying
as it was dying
the patient
bleeding in love
grew reminders
black as indelible
thrusting in distance
their one and only chance
to lock and chains

Street lights
change
narrow-minded bulbs
fickle as the sea
damp evening lounges
immune to moans
cruel as vacant
flushing out veins
and choice
drowned by crying
watches
the ferrymen jogging time
to its place in the clock

My houseful
garden stare
grew vacant in my fraying nerve
bald in our parting
torn before birth
the rapid seas
swept my moment bride
from the ring in my pine
leaving me
like a groom
printed on wallpaper
moated in my tumble-down squire and manor
lost
in pavement
disappearing
from the burnt ashes on our game
she
moved through the air
like a sum-total stranger
I couldn't
I wouldn't
I didn't
call her back
to play again the lyric in my sheet
though time
in its ruthless run
didn't offer us
too much to remember
was it so little
that you have forgotten
so soon

I SAW INTO THE GRAVE GRAVE

January 1972

I saw into the grave
grave
the day I first struck light
felt woe as time grew
clear
in the belfry
of my unmade brain
sucked
gall from the flooded tit
of a hanging cancer matron moon
grew
bitter in my flesh
as I grew hoarse in my throat
crying
vengeance in my mother-hold
drowning in tides of foam
across the fevered flowers of coming age

Struck dumb the mouthing
kisses
of my elders bending low
in love at cradle height
tore
the napkin from my crotch
placed a jock-strap
deep
in my challenged male
cursed God his choice
blasted
the blessed in his will

felt deep the mad world
clinging
to my wild worm
tried to claw from my
bone
the flesh of the world's laughter
somewhere in range
dug
tiny unmade fingers into chronicles
and heresies fit to break the will of Job
flung
fair the foul in my birth
across the sickroom of delivery
catching
the forceps on my chin
was counted out before the fight

Hanging low my cursed head
refused
to rise and breed dead maggots in my grain
burst my dumb egg
shedding
forsaken yoke on my firmament
freeing my tribe of creeping things
leading
them through doors
fit for angel wings

Lying helpless in my domain
hopeless
amongst shedded skin
I began to see my free end
around
the dark vagina of my death
find light where life was blind
feel
the solemn ground reach out
folding my growing choice
voicing
dead psalms to challenge the earth
to change my dwelling
place
and place
me again in some void
dreaming of nothing

In a parliament of my will

Still in my puppet
I see no end
other
than my own design

1972

Entwined
in steel
automatic
reliable
self-winding
in
jewelled limbs
hiding
biding time inside his clock

Living in no hour
by the minute hand of time
sharing
day lightning night with no one
nothing
moved by no one
nothing
but the seconds in his hard dial

Days in rush
night in flee
sadness in glee
years in rust

Trophies anchored in his stand
standing
in
alone
failures waved from his mast
waving
in
alone

Day lightning night in illuminous eyes
see nothing
remembers less

Nothing bared
nothing shared
only
the roaming hand
in his second-hand head

Bound to his own wrist
he
rarely sees
the face of his life
tho
he daily hears it ticking away

And

Losing count
of his thousands of millions of breath
hangs on
in his journeys speed
his golden deed
grows
solitary in patent
leaving
the remains of his brains
to cry
"cuckoo"
every hour

THERE ARE TOO MANY SAVIORS
ON MY CROSS
1972

There are too many saviors on my cross
lending their blood
to flood out my ballot box
with needs of their own
who put you there?
who
told you that was your place?

You carry me secretly naked in your heart
and clothe me publicly in armor
crying God is on our side
yet
I openly cry
who is on mine?
who
tell me who?
you who bury your sons and cripple your fathers
whilst you bury my father in crippling his son

The antiquated saxon sword
rusty in its scabbard of time now rises
you gave it cause in my name
bringing shame to the thorned head
that once bled for your salvation

I hear your daily cries
in the far-off byways in your mouth
pointing
north and south
and my calvary looms again
desperate
in rebirth
your earth is partitioned
but in contrition
it is the partition in your hearts
that you must abolish

You
nightly watchers of Gethsemane
who sat through my nightly trial
delivering me from evil
now deserted
I watch you share your silver
your purse rich in hate
bleeds my veins of love
shattering my bone
in the dust of the bogside and the shankhill road

There is no issue stronger
than the tissue of love
no need
as holy
as the palm outstretched
in the run of generosity
no monstrosity greater
than the acre you inflict

Who gave you the right to increase your fold?
and
decrease the pastures of my flock?
who gave you the right?
who gave it to you?
who?
and in whose name do you fight?

I am not in heaven
I am here
hear me
I am in you
feel me
I am of you
be me
I am with you
see me
I am for you
need me
I am all mankind
only through kindness
will you reach me

What masked
and bannered men
can rock the ark
and navigate a course
to their anointed kingdom come
who sailed their captain
to waters
that they troubled in my font?
sinking in the ignorant seas of prejudice

There is no virgin willing
to conceive in the heat
of any bloody sunday
you crippled children
lying in cries
on derry's streets
pushing your innocence
to the full flush face
of christian guns
(battling the blame on each other)
do not grow tongues
in your dying dumb wounds speaking my name
I am not your prize
in your death
you have exorcised me in your game of politics

Go home to your knees
and worship me in any cloth
as I was never tailor-made
who told you I was?
who gave you the right to think it?
take your beads
in your crippled hands
can you count my decades
take my love in your crippled hearts
can you count the loss

I am not orange
I am not green
I am a half-ripe fruit
needing both colors
to grow into ripeness
shame on you to have withered my orchard
I
in my poverty
alone
without trust
cry
shame on you
shame on you again and again
for
converting me into a bullet
and shooting me into men's hearts

The ageless legend of my trial grows old
in the youth of your pulse
staggering shamelessly from barricade to grave
filing in the book of history
my needless death one april
let me
in my betrayal
lie low in my grave
and you in your bitterness
lie low in yours
for our measurements grow strangely dissimilar

Our father who art in heaven
sullied be thy name

OUTSIDE THIS VASE

April 1972

Outside
this vase
flowers rise within

I
am out
side
the patch
lying on your page

it is from my eyes
that my seeds fall

wrinkled tears on parched world cheeks

blooming into your
eternal life-woman

Man hesitant
woman in speed
both
fuse the light life bulb
in my creation's lens

Did you grow in heat
together
lighting the world
on your voiced-out volumed
page?
was there rage in your appendage?

Male and female
exposed
in love
negative and positive
silently
springing your child
from its cave
into a pasture
of
unbroken lines

Crime is a shame
if shame
breaks light
blotting out
the meeting of holy
lips on blessed hair
echoing feelings
into
the right corridors of truth

Child's unborn hands
on grown-up hearts
unborn grown-up hearts
in the palms of children

Light reborn
in
the
corridors of the mind

Thoughts in shells
incubating
in first wonder
movement in vowels
circulating
the virgin inside her heir
transfixed
in form
cruciform in size
crucified in ears
unprepared
for nature

The first blood bleeds
the silent lips
each muscle
formed
pouted
in giving
holding
years
in
one
lifeday
spent in touch

The vase breaks
the seeds
fall
on the footprints
newly formed
on the earths sacred heart
bleeding
in
gladness
gliding our vocals
high
to the joy inside joy

Unchaining our growth
sentencing
our
life to the solitary confinement
inside
wisdoms
only
heart
beat

THE NEED I CONQUERED

April 1972

The need
I conquered
fed me stale
white crosses on my joy

bled all that cried
stuffed birds in flight
dried fruit before it died

The flesh
I needled
covered me thick
root blankets in my veins

grew seeds in wards
locked thighs in locks
tied tongues in kennelled cords

The life
I shed
planked wood across
the tender in my heart

shook paper hands
grew dust on grass
flew nettles in my lands

The death
I chose
paved me days
along remaining years

turned eyes to lies
fed tears to stone
flew vultures in my sighs

TIME IN MY BONDFIRE

1972

Time
in my bondfire
burns
my kingdom come

Time
bleeds my saviour merit
turns
upside down

Time
in my wildchild
yearns
outside in

Time
reeks
of
wreck

The infant bone
bursting
towards dust
shies clear the fluent flutter of dark
curses
the membrane mound moulding
the flesh without fight
slows
down the wandering wound

———

flowing from pus pore to sore shore
hears
the ghost of his orphan
silence the blessing out of sight
crying to his painted print of youth
turns
tissue into decay the day
the loud womb shut its door
heaving the cripple into decline

Time
sits
at
the
right
hand
awaits
its
chance
to
drown
alone
the
throne
of
the
ascension

Mourning
the birthday cake
the wake flung legs
across the life dance
tapping old rhythms
into the life of the burning born
home-made
his eyes plague the molten image
leaping into form feeding
veins the dried blood of graves
mouthing crowns the father mouthed
the day royalty left their soul
the graphic
in the clock winds
your jewelled speed
circumvents the pilgrimage
sells short the weight of the scale
voicing out the sailing prince
from the purpose of his palace
cradled
in lime
the child of magic
fostered in his box of tricks
lies
still
born

broken
before
the
wand
was
fully
weaved

Spring me
from
the
craggy crusted lips
of clay
that
drips
of time
awaiting to be kissed

EPILOGUE

FLANNY LAY

April 1972

Flanny lay

there

he lay there
lying where he lay

just there

knees under chin
arse against hip
curled
folded like a ball
refusing to unweave

just lay there

year after year after year

there

where he lay
on that point
recurring
like a dismal point recurring

just there

out of sight
bulging in his sac
refusing
to
unweave

Lay there where he lay lying
just
lying where he lay

Flanny
rested
there

awhile

year after year after year
passed

but

not by
not unnoticed

Flanny
waited
listened
knew

nothing had changed
really
changed

A hot line
through his navel
connected
to the stomach
of the world
transmitted
the outside wounded world
to his crib
Cain marked
the progress of the soil
and
Flanny wanted no acre of it

so

Long overdue
past
inducement
he starved himself
reduced
the bulge
pretended to disappear

He had been
immaculately conceived
now
he had been
immaculately de-conceived

so

he lay there
outside
outside pressure
and scalpel blade

just there

knees under chin
arse against hip
curled
folded like a ball
refusing to unweave

he was satisfied
in being dissatisfied
with
the sounds outside

so

he would
lie there
just there
where he lay

for a while

before unweaving
and
re-conceiving himself
in
a
world
of
his
own
head

ABOUT THE AUTHOR

RICHARD HARRIS was born in Limerick, Ireland, and studied to be an actor at the London Academy. After leaving the Academy, he made his debut in Joan Littlewood's production of Brendan Behan's *The Quare Fellow*, and this was soon followed by a part in Arthur Miller's play *A View from the Bridge*. Mr. Harris then toured Russia and Eastern Europe with Joan Littlewood's Theatre Workshop production of *Macbeth*, and subsequently began to act in films.

He is well known for his outstanding role in *This Sporting Life*, for which he received an Academy Award nomination and the Best Actor Award at the Cannes Film Festival. He has gained an international reputation for his acting in such films as *Camelot*, Antonioni's *The Red Desert*, *Hawaii*, and other films.

In the fall of 1970 he accepted an invitation to read some of his own poetry at the prestigious YM-YWHA Poetry Center in New York City. He has recorded a number of record albums, including "MacArthur Park"; and in March, 1972, he made his New York concert debut at Philharmonic Hall in Lincoln Center.

Mr. Harris has written a volume of short stories, *The Key in the Head*, soon to be published, and is just completing a novel, *Flanny At 1.10*.